Horizons

Phonics
& Reading K

Horizons

Phonics & Reading K

Book Two

Author
Guyla P. Nelson

Managing Editor

David J. Korecki

Consulting Editors

Sareta A. Cummins
Timothy E. Nelson

Editorial Assistants

Alan L. Christopherson
Jennifer L. Davis
Christine A. Korecki

Editor

John P. Robinett

Illustrators

Tye A. Rausch
Brian E. Stuck

Cover Design

Jonathan Chong
Mark Dinsmore
Brian E. Stuck

Alpha Omega Publications
Chandler, Arizona

Horizons Phonics & Reading K, Book Two is only a *part* of a complete kindergarten language arts curriculum which also includes spelling, writing, & vocabulary. It is *necessary* to use all of the teacher and student materials in the Horizons American Language Series for kindergarten in order to obtain a complete foundation in language.

Printed in the United States of America
ISBN 0-86717-982-1

① Put an X on each picture where you hear the **ẽr** sound.

ẽr				
ẽr				

② Circle the word your teacher reads.

1. sẽrf   sērġe   sẽrve

2. verb   Herb   her

3. clerk   jerk   perk

4. nerve   serve   swerve

5. term   fern   stern

3. Put an X on each picture that ends with the sound of **ẽr**.

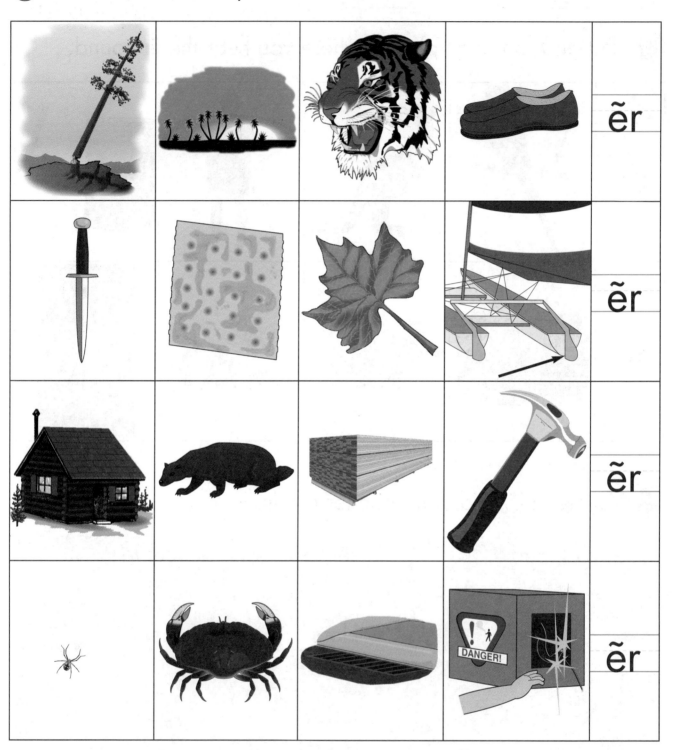

1   Put an X on each picture that ends with the sound of **ĕr**.

				ẽr
				ẽr
				ẽr
				ẽr

② Circle the middle vowel sound you hear.

ĕ ē ẽr		ĕ ē ẽr
ĕ ē ẽr		ĕ ē ẽr
ĕ ē ẽr		ĕ ē ẽr

③ Circle the word your teacher reads.

1.	hẽr	Hẽrb	vẽrb	pẽrch
2.	herd	kerf	serf	merge
3.	serge	verge	clerk	jerk
4.	perk	term	fern	kern
5.	stern	terse	verse	Bert

① Circle the word your teacher reads.

1.	kẽrn	stẽrn	tẽrse̸
2.	verse	Bert	pert
3.	nerve	serve	swerve

② Circle the vowel sound you hear in each picture.

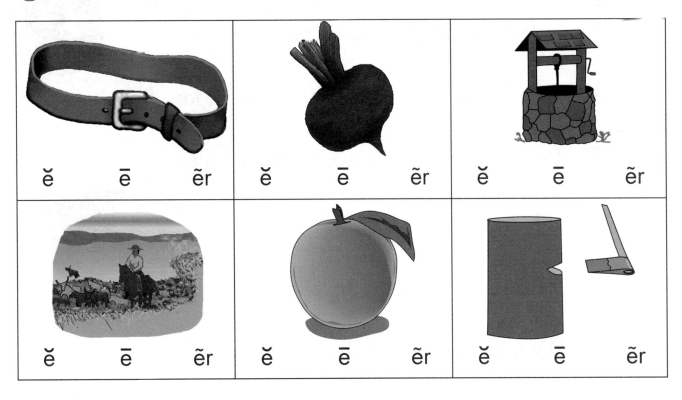

（3）Read the following sentences together.

1. Herb left his pen on the desk.

2. Did Dad catch a big perch?

3. Can we find the verb?

4. Ten men will drive the herd to the pen.

5. The cats and dogs were next to the fence.

6. Jack can tell who made the kerf.

7. In the old lands, a serf was a slave.

8. Frank wore his serge pants to the store.

9. The lads were at the verge of the cliff.

10. Is Fran a store clerk?

11. If we jerk the string, the kite can fall.

12. Dave told us to plant the fern by the gate.

1 Write the correct letter to finish each short vowel word.

1. c __ b   h __ t   p __ t

2. r __ t   n __ t   s __ t

3. c __ t   p __ n   j __ g

4. r __ d   b __ g   d __ ll

5. k __ ss   r __ n   c __ n

2 Write the correct letter to finish each Mother E word.

1. s __ fe   m __ le   m __ le

2. sn __ ke   sch __ me   p __ ne

3. ch __ ke   sh __ pe   r __ de

4. th __ me   h __ de   b __ le

5. h __ ge   h __ re   st __ ve

③ Look at the picture. Circle all items that have the **ẽr** sound.

① Draw a line between the word and its picture.

perch

kerf

serf

clerk

② Draw a line between the word and its picture.

jerk

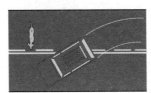

fern

serve

swerve

③ Read the following sentences together.

1. Did Tim watch the kern walk by?

2. Mom is still kind when she is stern.

3. That was a terse note.

4. Which verse did Gwen quote?

5. Bert spent his last dime in the store.

6. Jim did not jump when he lost his nerve.

7. Mom will serve cake to my pals.

8. Dad had to swerve to miss the pup.

1 Put an X on each picture where you hear the sound of **är**.

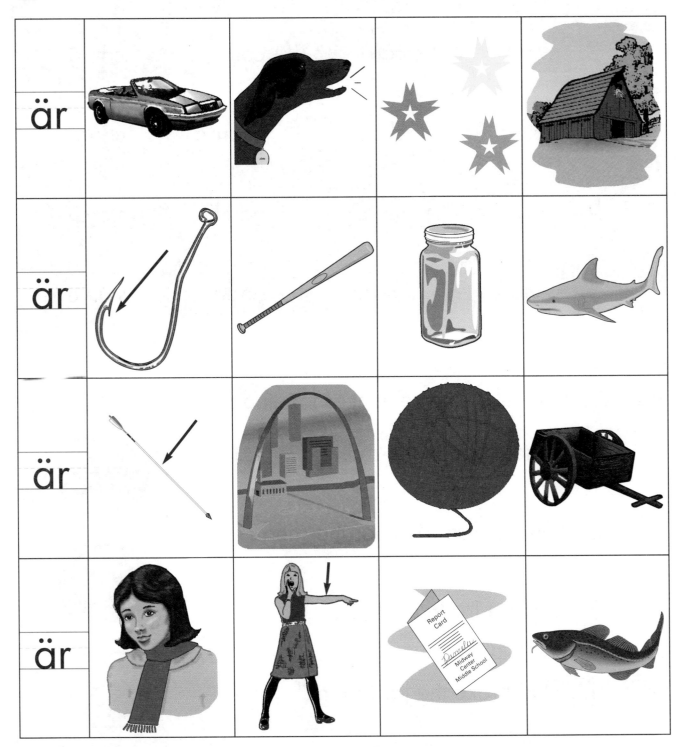

2 Circle the word your teacher reads.

1.	bär	bärb	bärk	Bärt
2.	car	card	cart	carve
3.	char	chard	charge	chart
4.	arch	march	parch	starch
5.	shark	sharp	smart	starve

3 Read the following sentences together.

1. Bruce rode in the red car.

2. The hot fire will char the shed.

3. It is not far to my home.

4. Dad broke the jar of jam.

5. Mark has a scar on his left leg.

Name _____

1 Put an X on each picture where you hear the sound of **är**.

är				
är				
är				
är				

② Circle the word your teacher reads.

1.	fär	färçe	färm	tärt
2.	star	stark	start	starve
3.	spar	spark	sparse	are
4.	scar	scarf	snarl	charm
5.	jar	mar	par	tar

③ Read the following sentences together.

1. The strong wind broke the spar of the ship.

2. Barb tore her sock on the barb of the fence.

3. The star is in its place in the sky.

4. We can note the huge arch from this place.

5. The black tar stuck to the tire.

1 Circle the middle vowel sound you hear.

ă	ā	är
ă	ā	är
ă	ā	är

ă	ā	är
ă	ā	är
ă	ā	är

2 Circle the word your teacher reads.

1. bärb   ḡärb   ärk   därk

2. bard   hard   lard   yard

3. barge   large   Marge   charge

4. hark   lark   mark   park

5. arm   charm   farm   harm

③ Circle the controlled vowel for the sound you hear.

är ẽr	 ar er	ar er
ar er	ar er	ar er

④ Read the following sentences together.

1. Can Barb drive the car?

2. Marge wore a red scarf.

3. Carl has a scar on his right arm.

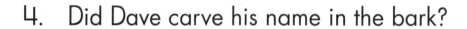

4. Did Dave carve his name in the bark?

5. Bert has a jar in the cart.

Name _____

1 Circle the controlled vowel for the sound you hear.

är ẽr	ar er	ar er
ar er	ar er	ar er
ar er	ar er	ar er

2 Circle the word your teacher reads.

1. tärn	bärn	yärn
2. carp	harp	sharp
3. dart	hart	mart

3 Read the following sentences together.

1. The men will march to the lake in March.

2. Mom will starch Dad's cuffs.

3. Are Mom and Dad at home?

4. Brent will sit in the back yard by the elm.

5. Is it hard to rake the grass?

4 Draw a line between the word and its picture.

car

card

carp

cart

1 Read the following rule and then listen for the **a̤r** sound.

> Rule 88:   After **w** or the **w** sound (**qu** or **squ**), **ar** has the sound of **ôr** as in **fôr**, and two dots are placed under **a̤r**.

Read the following words. Circle each word that has the **a̤r** sound.

1.	wa̤r	cär	wa̤rd	fär
2.	wa̤rm	wa̤rn	chärt	därt
3.	cärp	wa̤rp	wa̤rt	pärt
4.	yärd	scärf	wha̤rf	qua̤rt
5.	swa̤rm	färm	thwa̤rt	cärt

2 When Mother E follows the controlled vowel **ar**, she makes it say the "**air**" sound. Read each word and mark it like the examples given.

1.	bâre̸	flâre̸	râre̸	squâre̸
2.	blare	glare	scare	stare
3.	care	hare	share	tare
4.	dare	mare	snare	ware
5.	fare	pare	spare	scarce

3 Read the following sentences silently and then together with your teacher.

1. The shed was bare.

2. Save the rare dime.

3. Gene will stare at the sketch.

4. Did the harsh wind scare the lass?

5. Will Mike share his lunch?

6. It was fun to ride the mare.

7. Fresh milk is scarce in that land.

1 Put an X on each picture where you hear the sound of **ĩr**.

ĩr				
ĩr				
ĩr				

2 Circle the word your teacher reads.

1.	fĩr	sĩr	stĩr	whĩr
2.	birch	bird	third	dirge
3.	Kirk	quirk	shirk	smirk

③ Read the following sentences together.

1. Bert has on a red shirt.

2. Gert has a red shirt and black skirt.

3. Did the lad squirm as he sat?

4. Carl got dirt on his shirt.

5. This is her first farm.

④ Circle the word your teacher reads.

1.	swĩrl	twĩrl	whĩrl
2.	firm	squirm	first
3.	first	thirst	dirt
4.	shirt	skirt	squirt
5.	birth	mirth	thirst

1 Put an X on each picture where you hear the sound of **ĩr**.

2 Read the following sentences together.

1. Mom will stir the jam in the jar.

2. That is his third verse.

3. Did Dad plant a birch here?

Circle the middle vowel sound you hear.

ĭ ī ĩr	ĭ ī ĩr	ĭ ī ĩr
ĭ ī ĩr	ĭ ī ĩr	ĭ ī ĩr
ĭ ī ĩr	ĭ ī ĩr	ĭ ī ĩr

4 Read the following sentences together.

1. A red bird made a nest.

2. A dirge is a sad song.

3. The pop will squirt from the can.

1 Read the following sentences together.

1. Will Frank shirk his job?

2. Is it far to third base?

3. Her scarf will get dirt on it.

4. The milk will quench her thirst.

5. A large bird sat on the fence.

2 Circle the word your teacher reads.

1.	fĭt	fĭr	fīre
2.	fine	fir	firm
3.	first	fizz	file
4.	bide	bid	bird
5.	birch	bake	back

③ Write the correct letters to finish each word.

1. s ___ t   s ___ te   th ___ d

2. k ___ t   s ___ r   k ___ te

3. b ___ th   b ___ g   s ___ e

4. b ___ g   tw ___ l   b ___ ke

5. br ___ ke   b ___ nk   squ ___ t

④ Draw a line from the word to the correct picture.

birch

kirk

shirt

skirt

1　Put an X on each picture where you hear the sound of ĩr.

ĩr			
ĩr			

2　Read the following sentences together.

1. Mom will serve us first.

2. Did Bert swerve to miss the big fir?

3. A stern lad can twirl the pole.

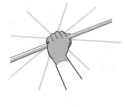

4. Rich will squirt his pal with a hose.

3 Look at the picture. Circle all items that have the **ĩr** sound.

Name _____

① Circle the controlled vowel for the sound you hear.

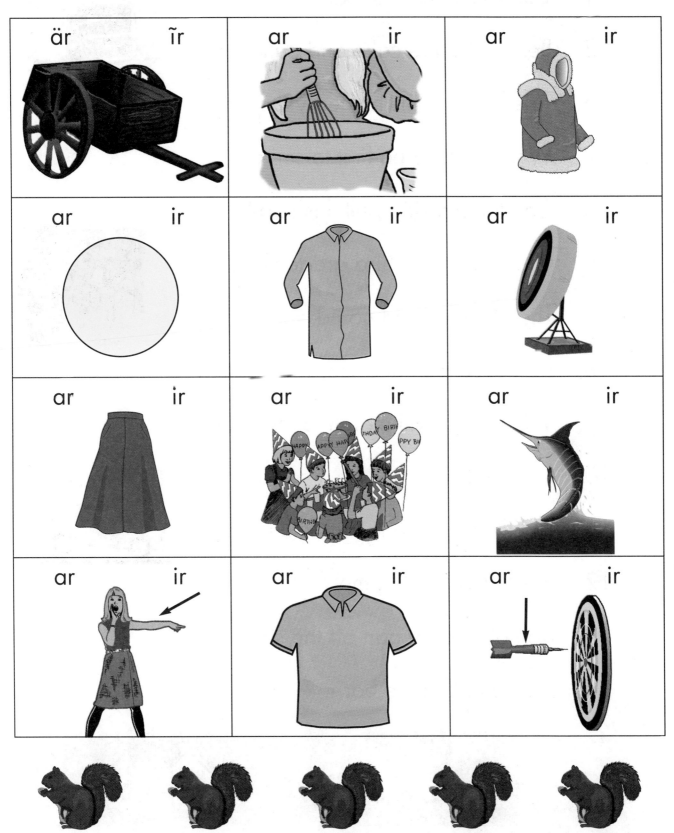

är ĩr	ar ir	ar ir
ar ir	ar ir	ar ir
ar ir	ar ir	ar ir
ar ir	ar ir	ar ir

2 Read the following sentences silently and then together with your teacher.

1. Can Merv start the car?

2. Bess will serve cake and punch.

3. This bird has his home by the marsh.

4. Who wants to be first to serve?

5. Can the big dog pull this cart?

6. Grace is in the third grade class.

7. The glass jar had no lid.

8. Do not scratch and mar the desk.

9. Which men will march to the lake?

10. Ask Jan to stir the jam.

11. Did Dad swerve to miss the bump?

12. Her hat will not fit me.

13. Do not jerk the pan off the stove.

14. Put the calf in the barn.

1 Put an X on each picture where you hear the sound of **ôr**.

ôr				
ôr				
ôr				
ôr				

② Circle the word your teacher reads.

1.	fôr	nôr	ôr
2.	torch	scorch	cord
3.	gorge	fork	cork
4.	stork	dorm	form
5.	norm	storm	born
6.	corn	horn	morn
7.	scorn	thorn	horse

③ Read the following sentences together.

1. Norm rode a black horse.

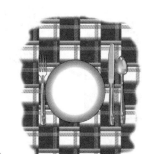

2. Dick fed corn to the pigs.

3. Jeff lit his torch.

4. The thorn will prick my hand.

5. Set the fork on the left side of the plate.

1 Circle the middle vowel sound you hear.

ŏ ō ôr	ŏ ō ôr	ŏ ō ôr
ŏ ō ôr	ŏ ō ôr	ŏ ō ôr
ŏ ō ôr	ŏ ō ôr	ŏ ō ôr
ŏ ō ôr	ŏ ō ôr	ŏ ō ôr

2 Read the following sentences together.

1. Did Jane scorch her dress?

2. Marge has a red cord on the shade.

3. Jack or Ned will drive the van.

4. Did Mom bake a cake for us?

5. A wind storm broke the pole.

3 Circle the word your teacher reads.

1.	shôrt	snôrt	sôrt
2.	short	sort	torte
3.	north	nor	norm
4.	for	fork	form
5.	cord	cork	corn

1 Circle the controlled vowel for the sound you hear.

är ẽr ôr	ar er or	ar er or
ar er or	ar er or	ar er or
ar er or	ar er or	ar er or
ar er or	ar er or	ar er or

② Read the following sentences together.

1. Jess will use his knife and fork.

2. Dad will lift the cork from the jug.

3. Bert held the torch in his hand.

4. A huge stork is on the lake.

5. Did his pet gorge on the nuts?

6. Jim will note the scorn on her face.

7. The thorn came from the red rose.

8. Is it morn yet?

9. Marge wore a short cape.

10. Did the horse snort?

1. After **w**, **or** can have the **er** sound and is marked **õr**. Read each word and mark it like the first one.

wõrd   worm

work   worse

world   worst

2. In the following words, **or** has a long **ō** sound. Mark each long vowel.

shōrn   port

torn   sworn

worn   force

fort

3 Look at the picture. Circle all items that have the **ôr** sound.

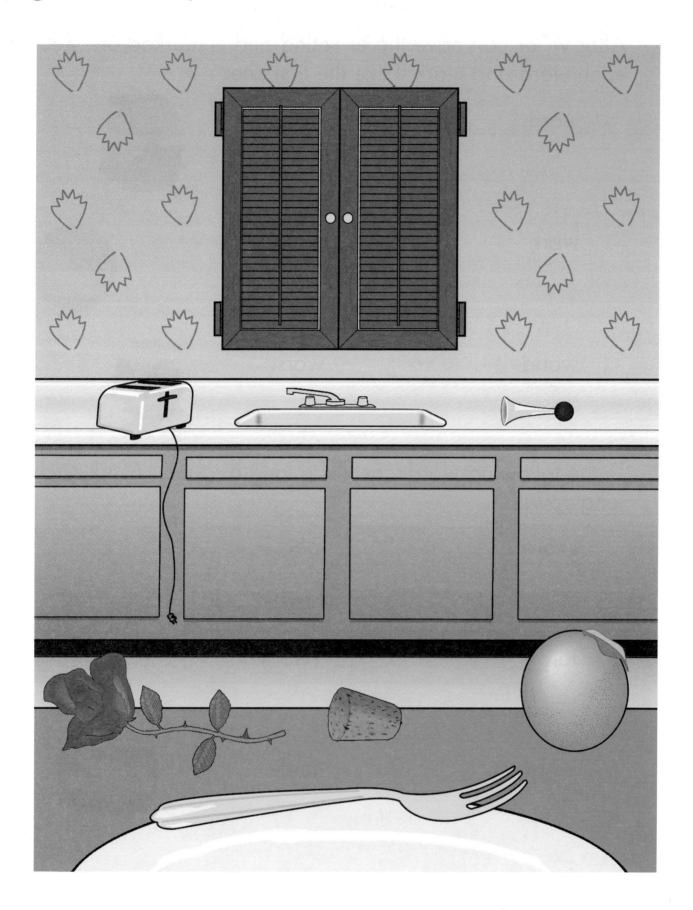

1 Put an X on each picture where you hear the sound of **ŭr**.

ũr				
ũr				
ũr				
ũr				

② Circle the word your teacher reads.

1. blũr	cũr	fũr	slũr
2. spur	curb	church	lurch
3. curd	surf	turf	burg
4. purge	surge	urge	lurk
5. murk	curl	furl	hurl

③ Read the following sentences together.

1. Will Jack have fun in the surf?

2. Mom will urge him to go.

3. The old ship will lurch in the storm.

4. The cat rubs its fur on the pole.

5. The bird was so high in the sky that it was just a blur.

1 Circle the controlled vowel for the sound you hear.

är ôr ũr	ar or ur	ar or ur
ar or ur	ar or ur	ar or ur
ar or ur	ar or ur	ar or ur
ar or ur	ar or ur	ar or ur

2 Circle the word your teacher reads.

1. bũrn	chũrn	spũrn	tũrn
2. urn	burnt	burp	slurp
3. burr	purr	nurse	curse
4. purse	burst	blurt	curt
5. hurt	spurt	curve	cur

3 Read the following sentences together.

1. Turn right at the next light.

2. The cat will purr if we give her milk.

3. The kind nurse held the sick lad in her arms.

4. Nan will take her red purse.

5. Sam hurt his leg when he fell.

1 Draw a line between the word and its picture.

spur

nurse

purse

curve

2 Read the following sentences together.

1. A nice girl will not slurp her milk.

2. The cold wind might burst the pipe.

3. The car must not take a fast curve.

4. Pete will hurl a rock at the snake.

5. Bruce will help Glen furl the flag.

Circle the middle vowel sound you hear.

ŭ	ū	ũr

ŭ	ū	ũr

ŭ	ū	ũr

ŭ	u̯	ũr

ŭ	u̯	ũr

ŭ	u̯	ũr

ŭ	ū	ũr

ŭ	ū	ũr

ŭ	ū	ũr

ŭ	ū	ũr

ŭ	ū	ũr

ŭ	ū	ũr

1 Circle the word your teacher reads.

1.	c͞ur	c͞urb	c͞url	c͞urt
2.	spur	spurn	slur	slurp
3.	burn	burnt	burp	burst
4.	blur	burg	blurt	burr
5.	turf	turn	church	churn

2 Read the following sentences together.

1. Jack wore a spur when he rode the horse.

2. Do not burn the trash!

3. Did the old folks live at the edge of the burg?

4. These lads like to run on the nice turf.

5. Bart and Ben will fly kites at the farm.

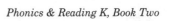

3 Look at the picture. Circle all items that have the **ŭr** sound.

1 Read the following together.

Vowel Digraphs #1

When two vowels go walking, the first vowel does the talking and says its long sound.

āi̸ as in quail   ōa̸ as in goat

āy̸ as in jay   ōe̸ as in hoe

ēa̸ as in teal   ōu̸ as in gourd

ēe̸ as in deer   ōw̸ as in crow

ēi̸ as in seize   ūe̸ as in hue

īe̸ as in pie   u̸e̸ as in glue

u̸i̸ as in fruit

2 Circle the vowel digraph for the sound you hear.

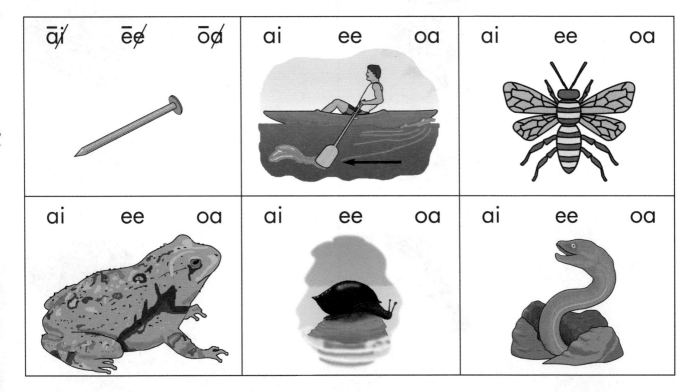

āi̸ ēe̸ ōa̸	ai ee oa	ai ee oa
ai ee oa	ai ee oa	ai ee oa

3 Circle the word your teacher reads.

1.	ā̸i̸d	brā̸i̸d	lā̸i̸d	mā̸i̸d
2.	paid	straight	ail	fail
3.	frail	hail	jail	mail
4.	nail	quail	rail	sail
5.	snail	tail	trail	hail

4 Draw a line from the word to the correct picture.

braid

tree

roach

train

knee

loaf

5 Circle the correct word for each picture.

~~jāil~~ ~~tāil~~ ~~trāil~~	~~feē~~ ~~seē~~ ~~teē~~	~~ōak~~ ~~sōak~~ ~~clōak~~
soar soap soak	waist wait quaint	seen seer seed
keen queen sheen	goat oat moat	frail fail tail
boat coat float	train trail trait	steep sleep sweep

6 Circle the word your teacher reads.

1. āim   claim   brain   chain

2. drain   gain   grain   lain

3. main   pain   plain   rain

4. slain   sprain   stain   strain

5. train   faint   paint   quaint

6. saint   taint   braise   praise

7. raise   waist   bait   gait

8. trait   wait   faith   maize

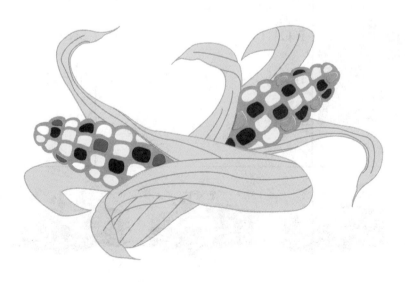

1 Circle the vowel digraph for the sound you hear.

ēē ōō āī	ee oa ai	ee oa ai
ee oa ai	ee oa ai	ee oa ai
ee oa ai	ee oa ai	ee oa ai
ee oa ai	ee oa ai	ee oa ai

2 Circle the word your teacher reads.

1. bee	fee	flee	free
2. glee	knee	see	tee
3. thee	three	tree	wee
4. whee	fleece	speech	screech
5. bleed	greed	creed	deed

3 Draw a line from the word to the correct picture.

fleece

float

frail

weed

load

maid

④ Circle the word your teacher reads.

1.	feed	freed	greed	heed
2.	need	seed	speed	tweed
3.	weed	beef	cheek	creek
4.	meek	peek	seek	week
5.	eel	feel	heel	kneel
6.	peel	steel	wheel	feel

⑤ Circle the correct word for each picture.

heel	sheep	sneer
steel	sleep	steer
wheel	steep	sheer

beet	sleet	sleeve
feet	sweet	sneeze
meet	sheet	squeeze

6 Circle the word your teacher reads.

1.	se̶e̶m	gre̶e̶n	te̶e̶n	scre̶e̶n
2.	beep	cheep	creep	deep
3.	keep	peep	seep	weep
4.	cheer	jeer	peer	queer
5.	cheese	fleet	greet	street
6.	tweet	breeze	freeze	wheeze

7 Read the following sentences together.

1. Do not sneeze on my sleeve.

2. Jim will squeeze my hand.

3. The deer will wade in the creek.

4. Is the creek deep?

5. The sleeve has a big rip in it.

6. Did you plant the seed?

1 Circle the vowel digraph for the sound you hear.

ō̶o̶ ā̶i̶ ē̶e̶	oa ai ee	oa ai ee
oa ai ee	oa ai ee	oa ai ee
oa ai ee	oa ai ee	oa ai ee
oa ai ee	oa ai ee	oa ai ee

2 Circle the word your teacher reads.

1. brōọch   cōọch   pōọch   rōọch

2. load   road   toad   loaf

3. cloak   croak   oak   soak

4. coal   goal   foam   roam

5. groan   loan   moan   soap

3 Draw a line from the word to the correct picture.

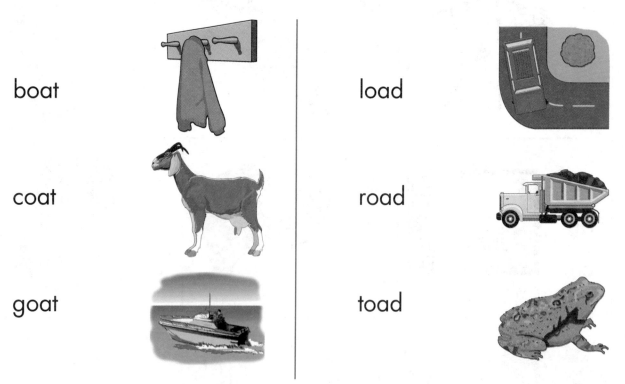

boat

coat

goat

load

road

toad

4 Circle the word your teacher reads.

1. ōọr	rōọr	sōọr	bōọrd
2. hoard	coarse	hoarse	boast
3. coast	roast	toast	bloat
4. boat	coat	float	goat
5. moat	oat	throat	oath
6. loathe	coax	hoax	whoa

5 Read the following sentences together.

1. Dad will coax Fran to sing.

2. This game is a hoax.

3. Tom ate a roast.

4. Bob will drive his car on the road.

5. Did Pam soak her coat?

6. A goat will climb the hill.

Draw a line to connect the words that rhyme.

week	wait	moan	drain
bait	boat	feel	groan
goat	peek	brain	heel

7 Circle the following words in the picture.

boat

coat

wheel

jeep

pail

tail

① Circle the vowel digraph for the sound you hear.

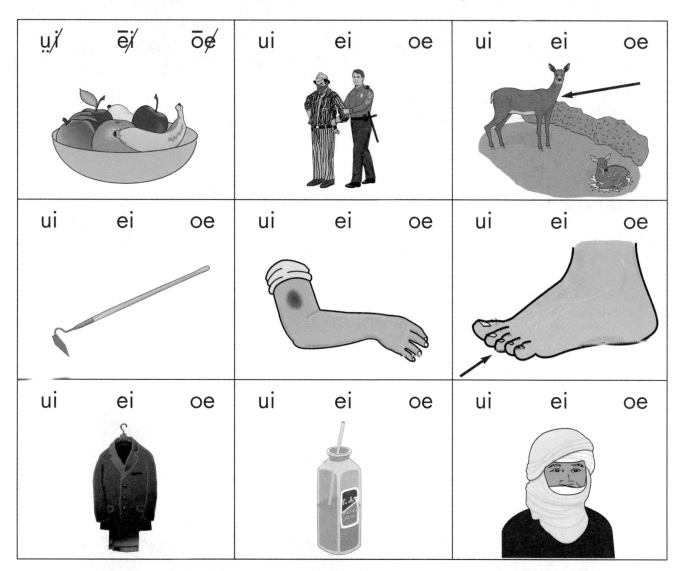

u~i~ e~i~ o~e~	ui ei oe	ui ei oe
ui ei oe	ui ei oe	ui ei oe
ui ei oe	ui ei oe	ui ei oe

② Circle the word your teacher reads.

1. juice   sluice

2. bruise   cruise

3. fruit   suit

③ Circle the word your teacher reads.

1.	wēȋrd	seize	sheik
2.	dōȩ	foe	goes
3.	hoe	toe	woe

④ Read the following sentences together.

1. I will drink a glass of juice.

2. Mom and Dad went on a cruise.

3. The men will seize the flag.

4. Joe likes to hoe the crops.

Name

1 Draw a line from the word to the correct picture.

hay

jay

pay

play

pray

spray

2 Circle the word your teacher reads.

1.	bāy̸	brāy̸	clāy̸	dāy̸
2.	fray	gray	hay	jay
3.	lay	may	nay	pay
4.	play	pray	ray	say
5.	slay	spray	stay	stray
6.	sway	tray	way	ray

3 Circle the correct word for each picture.

slay stay stray		sway way hay		bray gray tray	

4 Read the following sentences together.

1. Did the pup stray from home?

2. The wind will sway the branch.

3. Spray the paint on the desk.

4. Jeff will set his tray on the step.

5. Jill and Jack will play in the hay.

6. A jay sits on the limb.

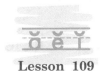
1 Circle the vowel digraph for the sound you hear.

ōw ūe̸ ēa̸	ow ue ea	ow ue ea
ow ue ea	ow ue ea	ow ue ea
ōw üe̸ ēa̸	ow ue ea	ow ue ea
		GLUE All Purpose
ow ue ea	ow ue ea	ow ue ea

②　Circle the word your teacher reads.

1.	blōw	bōw	crōw	flōw
2.	glow	grow	know	low
3.	low	mow	row	show
4.	slow	snow	stow	throw
5.	tow	owe	bowl	blown
6.	flown	grown	known	own
7.	shown	sown	grown	growth

③　Read the sentence.

A crow walks in the snow.

4 Draw a line from the word to the correct picture.

crow

throw

tow

5 Read the following sentences together.

1. Did Jack owe Jim a dime?

2. Fred ate a big bowl of fruit.

3. The wind has blown her hat off.

4. He fell in a snow drift.

5. The tow truck is red.

6. The growth of the plant is slow.

6 Circle the word your teacher reads.

1. c̲ū̲e̶   due   hue

2. clu̲e̶   blue   glue   true

7 Read the following sentences together.

1. The train is due at nine.

2. Will Frank give Jim the cue?

3. The rainbow has a nice hue.

4. Can glue fix it?

1 Circle the correct word for each picture.

bēạch blēạch prēạch	beak leak peak	seam steam stream
shear spear smear	reap heap leap	grease leash beast
bean dean lean	leaf leak leap	bead beak beard
peal meal real	heat seat neat	seam seat seal

2 Circle the word your teacher reads.

1.	flēa̸	pēa̸	plēa̸	sēa̸
2.	tea	peace	beach	bleach
3.	each	peach	preach	reach
4.	teach	bead	knead	lead
5.	plead	read	leaf	flea

3 Draw a line from the word to the correct picture.

peak

teal

beam

jeans

1 Draw a line to connect the words that rhyme.

bleak   real

heal   glean

cream   freak

clean   reap

cheap   dream

2 Draw a line between the word and its picture.

wreath

ear

weak

weave

③ Circle the word your teacher reads.

1.	bēak	crēak	lēak	pēak
2.	sneak	speak	squeak	streak
3.	tweak	weak	deal	heal
4.	meal	peal	real	seal
5.	squeal	steal	teal	veal
6.	zeal	beam	gleam	ream
7.	scream	seam	steam	team

④ Read the following sentences together.

1. The sand on the beach is hot.

2. The string broke and the beads fell on the rug.

3. A teal swims in the stream.

1 Draw a line to connect the words that rhyme.

dean	leap	please	feast
heap	shear	beast	leave
fear	crease	beat	tease
grease	lean	heave	heat

2 Draw a line from the word to the correct picture.

eat

 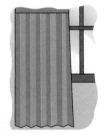

beat

pleat

wheat

③ Circle the word your teacher reads.

1. bēan   jēans   mēan   wēan

2. clear   dear   hear   near

3. rear   shear   smear   ear

4. spear   tear   year   beard

5. cease   crease   grease   ease

6. please   ease   tease   leash

7. east   least   bleat   cheat

8. eat   meat   neat   pleat

9. treat   wheat   breathe   weave

④ Read the following sentences together.

1. This year he will run in the race.

2. Dad will grease the truck.

3. A tear fell on his cheek.

4. Please help me lift the box.

5. It is not nice to tease a pal.

6. That beast is mean.

7. Jess hung the wreath on the tree.

① Draw a line from the word to the correct picture.

four

pour

gourd

court

② Circle the word your teacher reads.

1.	dŏu̸gh	th̲ōu̸gh	sōu̸l
2.	four	pour	source
3.	gourd	mourn	course
4.	court	fourth	four

③ Read the following sentences together.

1. Deb likes to knead the dough.

2. Though the sun shines, it may rain.

3. Dad did not mourn.

4. The king sat in his court.

5. Of course, we will go.

6. Chet is in fourth grade.

7. Who will pour the milk?

8. The wee tot slept till four.

9. Dave may plant a gourd by the step.

10. What was the source of the stream?

(1) Circle the word your teacher reads.

1. crīed	crīes	dīe	dīed
2. dies	dried	dries	flies
3. fried	fries	lie	lied
4. lies	pie	pies	pried
5. pries	shied	shies	skies
6. spied	spies	tie	tied
7. ties	tried	tries	tie

(2) Draw a line from the word to the correct picture.

pie

flies

tie

③ In a very few words ēy̸ appears to make the long ē sound. Connect the dots and then read the word below the picture.

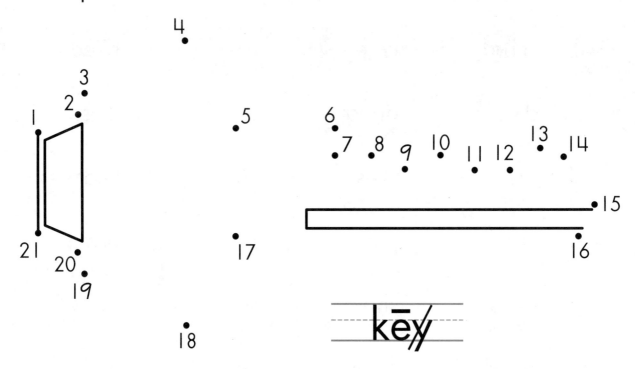

key̸

④ Read the following sentences together.

1. The score was a tie.

2. Six men tied a chain to the truck.

3. Four ties will be fine.

4. Frank pried the lid off the paint can.

5. The big dog spied the tan rat.

6. He tried to do his best.

7. She ate fries for lunch.

It Breaks the Rule!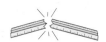

(1) These words break Rule 96 because **r** makes **ai** have the **âir** sound instead of long **ā**. Circle the correct word for each picture.

âir
châir
fâir

pair
air
hair

fair
stair
air

chair
pair
hair

chair
stair
fair

(2) Circle the word your teacher reads.

1.	âir	châir	fâir
2.	hair	pair	stair

It Breaks the Rule!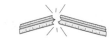

(3) These words break Rule 96 because the first vowel is not long. Instead, **ai** and **ay** make the short **ĕ** sound. Read the words and learn to spell and write them.

said   saith   says

It Breaks the Rule!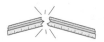

4 These words break Rule 4 because they make the hard **ḡ** sound before **e** instead of the soft **ġ** sound. Draw a line from the word to the correct picture.

gear

geese

5 Read the following sentences together.

1. See the wild geese in the sky!

2. Who broke my chair?

3. Will Mom curl her hair?

4. Sue says she will be here in June.

5. What saith the boss?

Name _____

It Breaks the Rule!

1 These words break Vowel Digraph #1 Rule 96. Here **r** controls the vowels. We hear the controlled vowel sound of **ẽr** since **a** is silent. Circle the correct word for each picture.

sẽarch pẽarl ẽarn		earn yearn earth	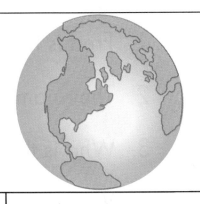
dearth earn learn		heard earn dearth	 learn earn search	

2 Read the following sentences together.

1. What did Frank earn for his work?

2. When did Jeff learn to write?

3. He paid a big price for the pearl.

5. Did Earl learn of earth and space?

It Breaks the Rule!

(3) These words break Vowel Digraph #1 Rule 96. Here **r** controls the vowels and we hear the "**air**" sound. Read each word and then write it. Read the sentences.

hêi̸r _____ | thêi̸r _____

1. Fred is heir to this tract of land.

2. Their names are not on this page.

3. Who is the right heir?

4. Will their price be right?

(4) When we add **s** to words that end in **r**, we hear the hard **s** sound. Read these words and sentences.

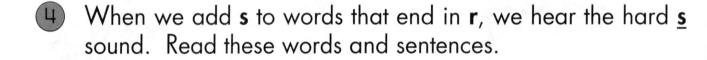

hêi̸r + s = hêi̸r**s**

their + s = theirs

1. Six heirs will claim this cash.

2. Is the cash theirs?

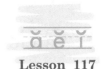
1 Read the following together.

Vowel Digraphs #2

When two vowels go walking, the first vowel does the talking but does not say its long sound.

au̶ as in sauce   ăi̶ as in plaid

aw as in law   ău̶ as in laugh

ĕa̶ as in bread   ĭe̶ as in sieve

ei̶ as in sleigh   ôa̶ as in broad

ey̶ as in they   ȯe̶ as in does

ôu̶ as in bought   oe̶ as in shoe

ĕi̶ as in heifer

ĕa̶ as in leopard

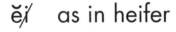

(2) Circle the word your teacher reads.

1. sauce	caught	taught
2. haul	fault	launch
3. haunt	cause	pause

(3) Draw a line from the word to the correct picture.

caught

haul

launch

sauce

(4) Read the following sentences together.

1. Did Claude pause when he spoke?

2. Maude caught the ball.

3. Paul caught a fish.

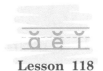
1 Circle the correct word for each picture.

dawn lawn yawn	claw draw flaw	dawn drawn fawn
gnaw jaw law	paw raw slaw	sprawl trawl crawl
yawn fawn drawn	squaw straw thaw	shawl squawk hawk

A hawk will make the hen squawk.

② Circle the word your teacher reads.

1.	claw	draw	flaw	gnaw
2.	jaw	law	paw	saw
3.	slaw	squaw	straw	thaw
4.	hawk	squawk	crawl	shawl
5.	sprawl	trawl	dawn	drawn

③ Read the following sentences together.

1. Dawn has a red and white shawl.

2. I did not see Claude yawn.

3. The cat will claw the tree.

4. I will draw a boat that has a sail.

5. Jack Shaw had slaw for lunch.

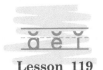
1 Circle the correct word for each picture.

br~~e~~ad d~~e~~~~a~~d dr~~e~~ad	lead head read	cleanse meant spread
threat thread tread	health deaf wealth	sweat death breath

2 What kind of bird is this? Can you read his name? Remember—**ph** says **f**.

pheasant

③ Read the following sentences together.

1. Can the deaf man sing?

2. Dad meant for Dave to sing.

3. Mom put fresh bread on my plate.

4. Jan will spread jam on the roll.

5. The man will sweat as he digs the huge hole.

6. The stern man was a threat to the wee lad.

7. Fresh air will help his health.

8. Sis will use red thread to mend the dress.

9. When did the man earn his wealth?

10. Did Joe bump his head?

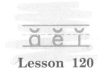
① In the following words, **eị** makes the sound of long **ā**.
Circle the word your teacher reads.

1. ne_i_gh   sl_ei_gh   we_i_gh

2. eight   freight   weight

3. veil   rein   vein

② Draw a line between the word and its picture.

sleigh

eight

veil

vein

3 Read the following sentences together.

1. Dale rode in the sleigh.

2. The weight of the truck is two tons.

3. Jane will hold the reins as she rides the horse.

4. Did Joe cut the vein in his leg?

5. The horse will neigh as it pulls the sleigh.

1 In the following words, <u>e</u>y̸ makes the sound of long ā. Read the words and then read the sentences.

hey _____

they _____

prey _____

whey _____

1. Hey! Did Jan see that?

2. They went by the lake to see a boat.

3. Did the cat catch its prey?

4. Mom will put the whey in a can.

5. Will they leave us here?

6. They saw ten fish in a pan.

Did the fox catch its prey?

② Listen for the sound of **ôʉ** in the following words.

bôʉght   ôʉght

brought   sought

fought   thought

③ Read the following sentences together.

1. A man sought for the lamb till dark.

2. Shane thought he brought it home.

3. Frank fought to keep the huge dogs off.

4. Pam bought a green coat.

5. We ought to leave by ten.

1 Read each word and then write it. Read the sentences.

plăĭd _____ | brôŏd _____

The girl wore a plaid hat.   The river is broad.

2 Read each word and then write it. Read the sentences.

sĭĕvĕ _____ | lăŭgh _____

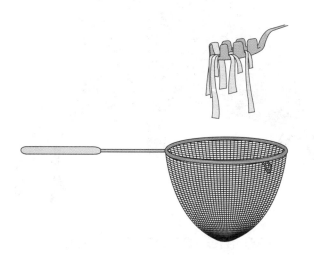

Strain it with the sieve.   It is fun to laugh.

3 Read each word and then write it. Read the sentence.

dȯe̸s _____ | shȯe̸ _____

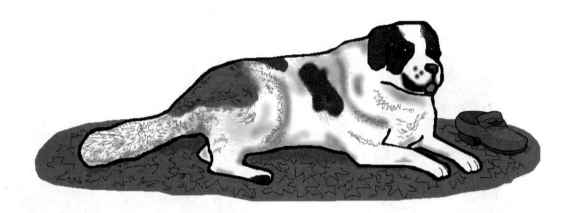

Does he have an old shoe?

4 Read each word and then write it. Read the sentences.

hĕi̸fẽr _____ | lĕo̸pãrd _____

The heifer will run. See the leopard sleep.

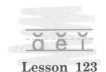

1 Read the following together.

Vowel Digraphs #3

When two vowels go walking, the second vowel does the talking and says its long sound.

e̶ā as in gre̶āt   e̶w̶ as in scre̶w̶

e̶ī as in he̶īght   e̶ȳ as in e̶ȳe̶

e̶ū as in fe̶ūd   i̶ē as in chi̶ēf

e̶u̶ as in sle̶u̶th   o̶u̶ as in so̶u̶p

e̶w̄ as in ste̶w̄   u̶ī as in gu̶īde

u̶ȳ   as in bu̶u̶ȳ

2 Read the sentence.

Did the ball break the pane?

3 Circle the word your teacher reads.

1.	br~~e~~āk	st~~e~~āk	gr~~e~~āt	y~~e~~ā
2.	great	steak	yea	break
3.	height	sleight	steak	great

4 Read the following sentences together.

1. What is his height?

2. Yea! Mom will serve us steak.

3. This is a great day!

4. We had steak at lunch.

5. Grace will not break the string.

6. He did the trick by sleight of hand.

1 Read the word and then write it. Connect the dots.

e̶ū   feud

Who will win the feud?

2 Read the word and then write it. Color the picture.

ĕu   sleuth   _____

The sleuth will catch the thief.

1 Read the word and then write it.

e͟w   mew

2 Circle the word your teacher reads.

1.	dew	few	hew	knew
2.	mew	new	pew	spew
3.	stew	whew	news	newt

3 Draw a line from the word to the correct picture.

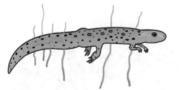

pew

hew

newt

④ Circle the word your teacher reads.

1.	bl~~e~~w	br~~e~~w	ch~~e~~w
2.	crew	drew	flew
3.	grew	screw	threw

⑤ Read the following sentences together.

1. Dirk threw a large stone.

2. The birds flew from the North when it got cold.

3. Mom will brew a pot of tea.

4. Place a screw here.

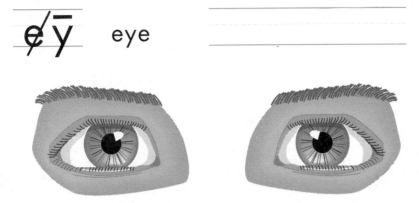
1 Read the word and then write it.

e̸ȳ̄   eye

2 Circle the correct word for each picture.

nîēçé / pîēçé	brief / chief	grief / thief
field / shield	shield / yield	fierce / pierce
yield / piece	tier / pier	brief / shriek

③ Circle the word your teacher reads.

1.	niece	piece	brief	chief
2.	grief	thief	shriek	field
3.	shield	yield	fierce	pierce
4.	priest	piece	pierce	grief

④ Read the following sentences together.

1. Big Chief likes it here.

2. Let me walk in the field.

3. A fierce wind blew all night.

4. The thief took my bike.

5. Please eat a piece of cake.

1 Read the word and then write it. Read the sentence.

ǿṳ̈   soup

I like Mom's hot soup for lunch.

2 Circle the word your teacher reads.

1.	yǿṳ̈	yǿṳ̈r	yǿṳ̈rs	yǿṳ̈th
2.	through	group	soup	you
3.	tour	route	your	group
4.	you	through	your	tour

3 Read the following sentences together.

1. Please put your list on the desk.

2. Which route will we take?

3. Will you go with me?

4. We will eat soup for lunch.

5. Beth has a deep wound.

6. He came through the storm.

4 Read the following sentences together.

1. Please go on the tour with Sam.

2. A group left at six.

3. Is this bike yours?

4. The troupe will put on a play.

5. Dave is a tall youth.

1 Read the word and then write it.

ŭ ī   guide   _____

2 Help the dog get the man home through the maze.

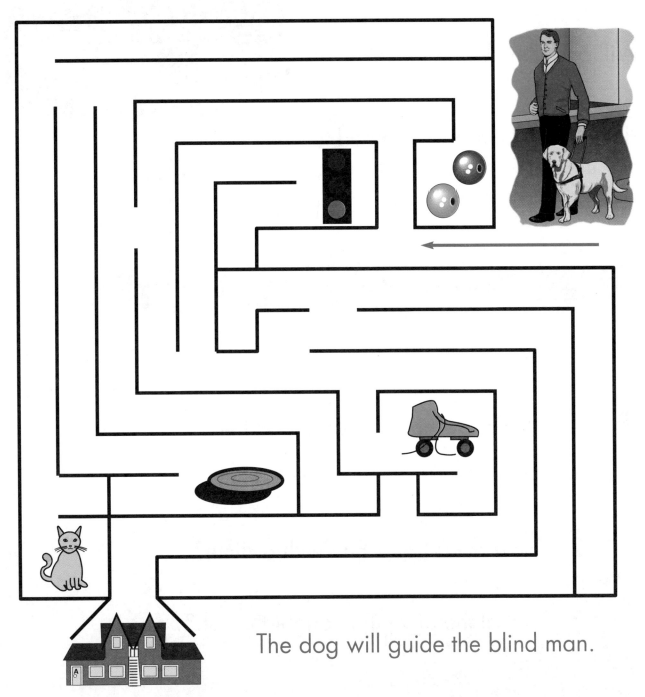

The dog will guide the blind man.

3 Read the word and then write it. Read the sentences.

 buy _____

The guy wants to buy one piece for a dime.

Will one dime buy a piece?

How many dimes will he need to buy the mint? Put an X on the coins that he will need.

$ .30

4 Read the following sentences together.

1. The chief will guide us to his hut.

2. How much can I buy with a dime?

3. Is that the guy who caught the fish?

① Read the following together.

Vowel Digraphs #4

When two vowels go walking, the second vowel does the talking and says its short sound.

i̸ĕ as in friend   u̸ĕ as in guess

o̸ŭ as in touch   u̸ĭ as in build

a̸ĭ as in captain   e̸y̆ as in chimney

e̸ĭ as in forfeit   u̸ă as in guarantee

② Read the word and then write it. Read the sentence.

i̸ĕ   friend   _____

Can we be friends?

Read the word and then write it. Read the sentence.

o̸ŭ   touch   _____

Do not touch!

4 Choose the correct word to finish each sentence and write it on the line.

rough / tough

1. The road is _____ .

rough / tough

2. Is the meat _____ ?

tough / touch

3. Do not _____ the hot stove.

young / rough

4. The _____ lad must run fast.

1. Read the word and then write it. Read the sentence.

ǔě guess _____

Guess what you can see in the circles.

2. Choose the correct word to finish each sentence and write it on the line.

guess / guest

1. Can you _____ my name?

guess / guest

2. The girl is my _____ .

Guess / Guest

3. _____ which string is short.

guess / guest

4. Please be my _____ for lunch.

③ Read the word and then write it.

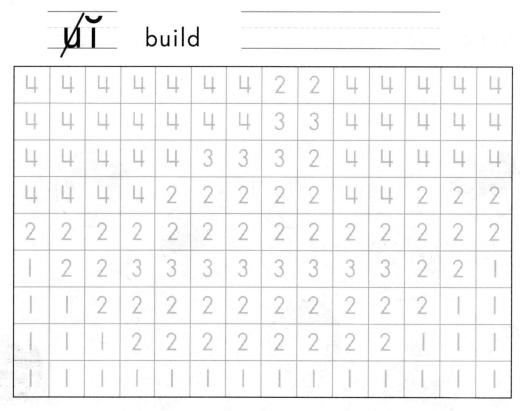

ʊ̃Ĭ̃   build   _____

Use these colors to build a boat with blocks at the art guild.

1. Dark Blue   2. Black   3. Red   4. Light Blue

④ Choose the correct word to finish each sentence and write it on the line.

build / guild

1. We will help Dad _____ a shed.

build / guild

2. Mom met with the art _____ .

built / guilt

3. He _____ his home by a lake.

built / guilt

4. Can the judge tell his _____ ?

It Breaks the Rule!

1 These words break Vowel Digraph #4 Rule 99. Note that **r** controls the vowels and makes them say the "**air**" sound. The first vowel ȩ is silent. Circle the correct word for each picture.

pȩâr bȩâr tȩâr		swear wear tear	
wear tear bear		bear pear swear	

2 Read the following sentences together.

1. Josh will wear a red shirt.

2. Did Jake tear his hat?

3. May we eat the ripe pear?

4. Did a bear cross her path?

3 In these words **r** controls e̸ä and makes the vowels say the **är** sound.

he̸ärt	he̸ärth

4 Circle the correct word for each picture.

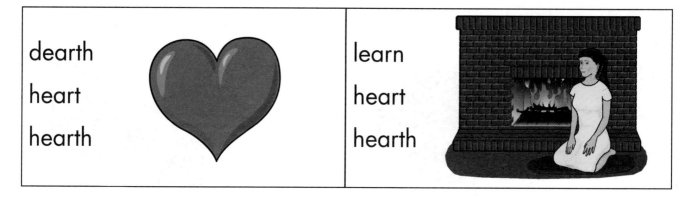

dearth
heart
hearth

learn
heart
hearth

5 Read the following sentences together.

   1.   Do you love with all your heart?

   2.   Pat and Dale sat by the hearth to read.

1 Read the following together.

Vowel Digraphs #5
(Special)

These are special because **o** and **o** go walking and both vowels do the talking.

o͝o as in book   o͞o as in goose

2 Circle the word your teacher reads.

1.	g͞o͞od	ho͝od	sto͝od	wo͝od
2.	book	brook	cook	crook
3.	hook	look	nook	shook
4.	took	wool	foot	soot

The dog shook the book.

3 Read the following sentences together.

1. Take a good look at this book.
2. Who took my wool hood?
3. Jed stood at the edge of the pond.
4. Hear the brook sing!
5. Look at the crook in that rod!
6. Clean the soot off the bench.
7. The nook is a good spot to sit and read.
8. Did they cook the meat in a big pot?
9. Put the wood by the back fence.
10. Hang your coat on the hook, please.

4 Draw a line from the word to the correct picture.

hood

brook

wool

foot

1 Circle the word your teacher reads.

1.	bōo	cōo	mōo	tōo
2.	zoo	brood	food	mood
3.	goof	hoof	proof	roof
4.	cool	drool	fool	pool
5.	school	spool	stool	tool

2 Read the following sentences together.

1. Did the cow moo?

2. Will the roof leak when it rains?

3. We went to the zoo.

4. The cat will play with the spool on the rug.

③ Draw a line from the word to the correct picture.

goose

groom

school

stool

④ Circle the word your teacher reads.

1. bloom	boom	broom	gloom
2. groom	loom	room	zoom
3. loon	moon	noon	soon
4. spoon	coop	droop	hoop
5. loop	scoop	snoop	stoop

1 Draw a line from the word to the correct picture.

loom

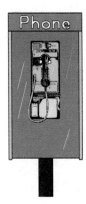

bloom

loop

booth

2 Choose the correct word to finish each sentence and write it on the line.

boom / bloom

1. The rose will _____ soon.

boom / broom

2. Use the _____ to sweep the step.

scoop / snoop

3. Mom will give me a _____ of ice.

shoot / scoot

4. Dad will _____ his gun.

boot / toot

5. My _____ has mud on it.

③ Draw a line from the word to the correct picture.

scoop

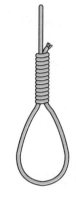

boot

noose

root

④ Circle the word your teacher reads.

1. troop   poor   choose   goose

2. loose   moose   noose   boost

3. roost   boot   hoot   root

4. scoot   shoot   toot   booth

5. tooth   smooth   soothe   groove

1 Choose the correct word to finish each sentence and write it on the line.

booth / tooth

1. I broke my _____ when I fell.

ooze / snooze

2. The mud will _____ by his big toe.

ooze / snooze

3. Watch the dog _____ by the fire.

boost / boot

4. Dad will _____ me up so that I can see the band go by.

root / roost

5. The hen will _____ on the ledge.

2 Draw a line from the word to the correct picture.

zoo

moose

broom

3 Circle the vowel digraph for the sound you hear.

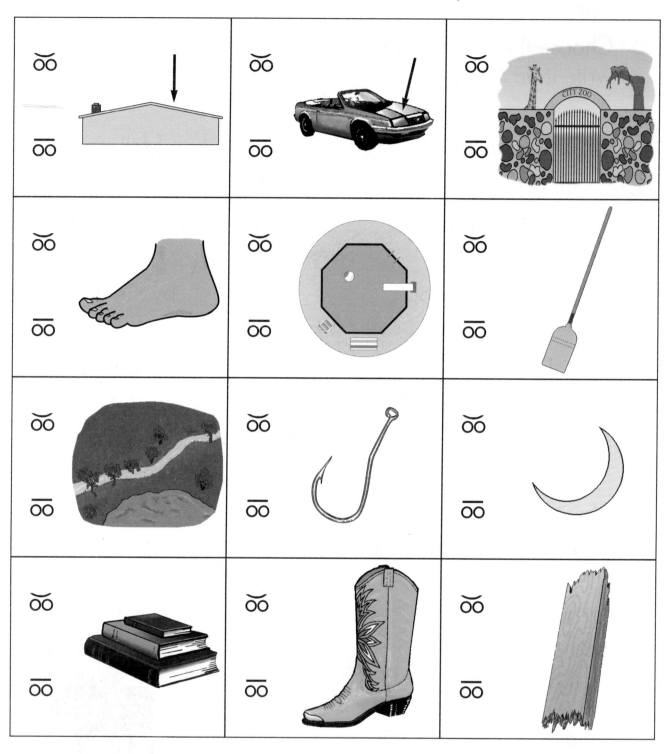

The owl will hoot.

1 Circle the vowel digraph for the sound you hear.

o͝o o͞o	o͝o o͞o	o͝o o͞o
o͝o o͞o	o͝o o͞o	o͝o o͞o
o͝o o͞o	o͝o o͞o	o͝o o͞o
o͝o o͞o	o͝o o͞o	o͝o o͞o

It Breaks the Rule!

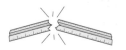

② These words break Rule 100 because **oo** does not make either of the sounds for Vowel Digraph #5. Listen as your teacher reads each word and then write it.

blood _____

flood _____

door _____

floor _____

③ Circle the word your teacher reads.

1. blood	flood	wood	food
2. food	flood	hood	good
3. wood	stood	blood	brood

④ Read the following sentences together.

1. The life of the flesh is in the blood.

2. Much rain may cause a great flood.

3. The strong lad got blood on his shirt.

4. Dad wants to put a new floor in this room.

5. The girls will please come through this door.

① Read the following together.

Diphthong

In a **diphthong** two vowels go walking together in the same syllable, and both vowels are sounded together.

oi as in oink   **ou** as in ouch

oy as in toy   **ow** as in cow

② Read the word and then write it. Read the rule.

oi   oink

When the "**oi**" sound comes at the first or
in the middle of the word, we spell it **oi**.

③ Draw a line from the word to the correct picture.

boil

coil

foil

oil

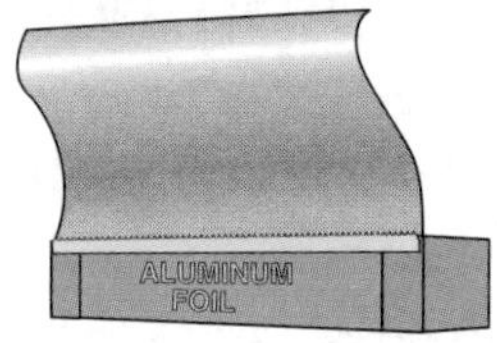

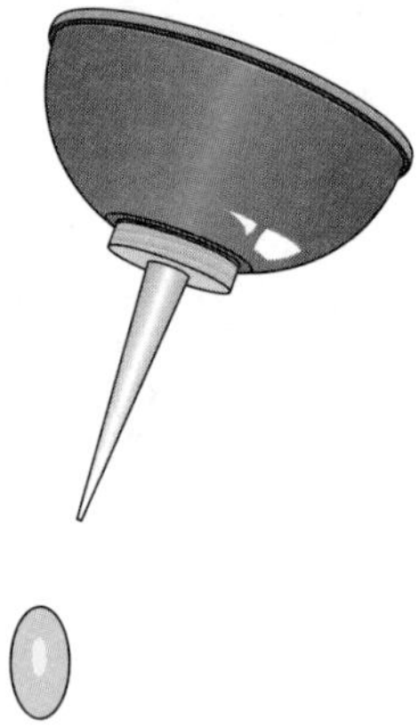

④ Circle the word your teacher reads.

1.	choice	voice	boil
2.	broil	coil	foil
3.	oil	soil	spoil
4.	toil	coin	join
5.	joint	point	noise
6.	hoist	moist	oink

1 Draw a line from the word to the correct picture.

coin

joint

point

hoist

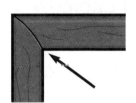

2 Draw a line to connect the words that rhyme.

choice

boil

coin

joint

hoist

foil

point

moist

voice

join

3 Read the following sentences together.

1. He spoke in a clear voice.

2. We will broil the steaks for lunch.

3. Jake and Sam will coil the rope.

4. Mom will wrap the lamb chops in foil.

5. The harsh noise woke the wee tot.

6. Please give us a choice.

7. Will you join us for lunch?

Will you give me a coin?

1 Read the word and then write it. Read the sentence.

oy toy

Roy will wash a toy and Troy will jump for joy.

2 When the "**oi**" sound comes at the end of a word, we use **oy**. Read each word and then write it.

boy

joy

soy

toy

Joy

Roy

Troy

coy

3 Read the following sentences together.

1. Roy and Troy hid the toy.

2. The first boy to cross this line will win.

3. His heart is full of joy.

4. We like the soy sauce on this food.

The Heart of a Boy

I have breakfast, dinner, tea:
And everyone is good to me:
    But somewhere, in another street,
    There isn't even bread to eat.

Can't I share what's given me?
Half my dinner? Half my tea?
    Half my sweets and half my toys?
    "Yes," says Dad, "and half your noise."

1 Read the word and then write it. Read the rule.

ou   mouse

The "**ou**" sound is usually spelled **ou** unless it comes at the end of a word or before **l** or **n**.

2 Draw a line from the word to the correct picture.

couch

pouch

cloud

pounce

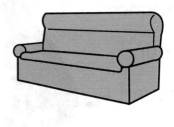

3 Circle the word your teacher reads.

1.   couch   crouch   grouch   ouch

2.   pouch   slouch   cloud   loud

3.   proud   gouge   bounce   flounce

4.   ounce   pounce   bound   found

5.   ground   hound   mound   pound

4 Circle the correct word for each picture.

hound round sound	douse grouse mouse	mouse blouse house
sprout stout trout	mouth south scout	shout snout spout

1 Draw a line from the word to the correct picture.

ouch

spout

mouse

blouse

2 Circle the word your teacher reads.

1.	round	sound	wound	lounge
2.	count	fount	mount	flour
3.	hour	our	scour	sour
4.	douse	grouse	house	mouse
5.	blouse	doubt	grout	out

③ Choose the correct word to finish each sentence and write it on the line.

couch / grouch

1. I will not be a _____ .

mouth / south

2. The wind blew from the _____ .

mouth / mount

3. The food is in his _____ .

sprout / shout

4. Did the beans _____ ?

sprout / shout

5. Do not _____ in the house.

④ Draw a line to connect the words that rhyme.

pout   house

mouth   sprout

mouse   south

 ① Circle the correct word for each picture.

count fount mount		out pout rout	
scout shout spout		count fount mount	

② Circle the word your teacher reads.

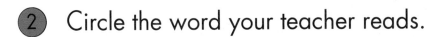

1. out   pout   rout

2. scout   shout   snout

3. spout   sprout   stout

4. trout   mouth   south

③ Choose the correct word to finish each sentence and write it on the line.

sprout / trout

1. Dad and Frank will catch _____ .

ground / hound

2. The seeds fell on good _____ .

grouse / grout

3. Fred and Chet will hunt for _____ .

wound / round

4. We _____ the kite string on a stick.

wound / round

5. The earth is _____ .

bounce / pounce

6. Let us _____ the ball.

④ Draw a line from the word to the correct picture.

hound   flour   trout   ground

① Read the word and then write it. Read the rule.

OW cow

The "**ou**" sound is usually spelled **ow** when it comes at the end of a word or before **l** or **n**.

② Draw a line from the word to the correct picture.

cow

plow

fowl

growl

3 Circle the word your teacher reads.

1. bow	brow	chow	cow
2. how	now	plow	prow
3. sow	vow	wow	crowd
4. cowl	fowl	growl	howl
5. jowl	owl	prowl	scowl

4 Draw a line from the word to the correct picture.

clown

crown

gown

town

1. Draw a line between the word and its picture.

bow

sow

owl

frown

2. Circle the word your teacher reads.

1.	prowl	yowl	scowl
2.	brown	clown	crown
3.	down	drown	frown
4.	gown	town	down
5.	browse	drowse	crowd

3 Read the following sentences together.

1. It is not good to frown.

2. Ted has a pair of brown pants.

3. Wow! What a big crowd!

4. The black and white cow gives us milk.

5. Russ will plow this field in May.

6. Jack fell down and broke his crown.

4 Circle the correct word for each picture.

cow chow bow	plow prow prowl	scow owl sow
cowl owl fowl	crown cowl clown	gown down town

It Breaks the Rule!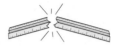

1 This word breaks Rule 106 because the **ou** sound is not spelled **ow** at the end of a word. Listen as your teacher reads the word and then write it.

thou _____

It Breaks the Rule!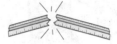

2 These words break Rule 105 because **ou** comes before **l** or **n** instead of **ow** before **l** or **n**. Listen as your teacher reads the word and then write it.

foul _____ | noun _____

3 Read the following sentences together.

1. Thou art my friend.

2. That ball is a foul.

3. A noun is a word that names.

4. Look at the picture. Circle all items that have the **oi**, **oy**, **ou**, or **ow** sounds.

1 Circle the correct letter for the beginning consonant sound.

l d c t	l d c t	l d c t
l d c t	l d c t	l d c t
l d c t	l d c t	l d c t
l d c t	l d c t	l d c t

Circle the correct letter for the beginning consonant sound.

f v w s	f v w s	f v w s
f v w s	f v w s	f v w s
f v w s	f v w s	f v w s
f v w s	f v w s	f v w s

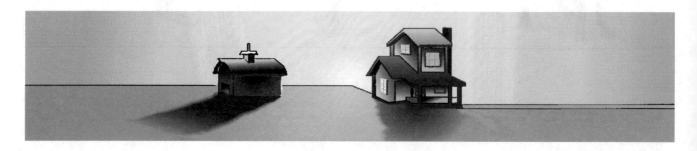

1 Circle the correct letter for the beginning consonant sound.

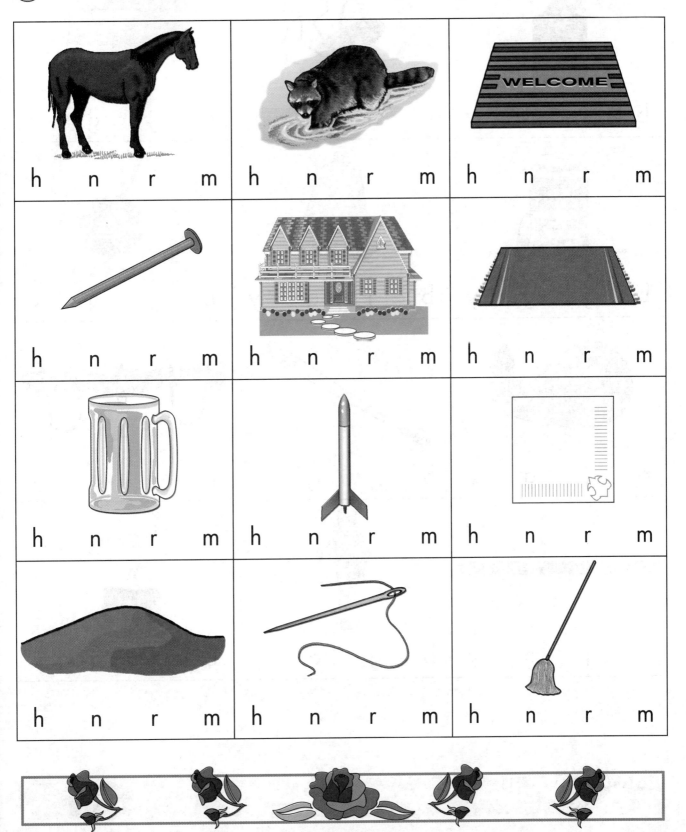

h n r m	h n r m	h n r m
h n r m	h n r m	h n r m
h n r m	h n r m	h n r m
h n r m	h n r m	h n r m

Circle the correct letter for the beginning consonant sound.

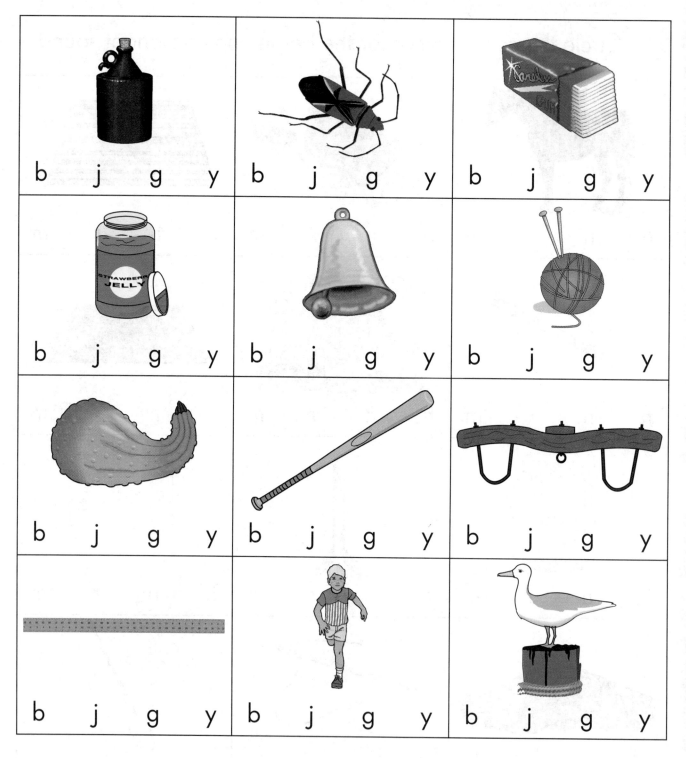

b j g y	b j g y	b j g y
b j g y	b j g y	b j g y
b j g y	b j g y	b j g y
b j g y	b j g y	b j g y

(1) Circle the correct letter for the beginning consonant sound.

p qu k z	p qu k z	p qu k z
p qu k z	p qu k z	p qu k z
p qu k z	p qu k z	p qu k z
p qu k z	p qu k z	p qu k z

2 Circle the correct letter for the ending consonant sound.

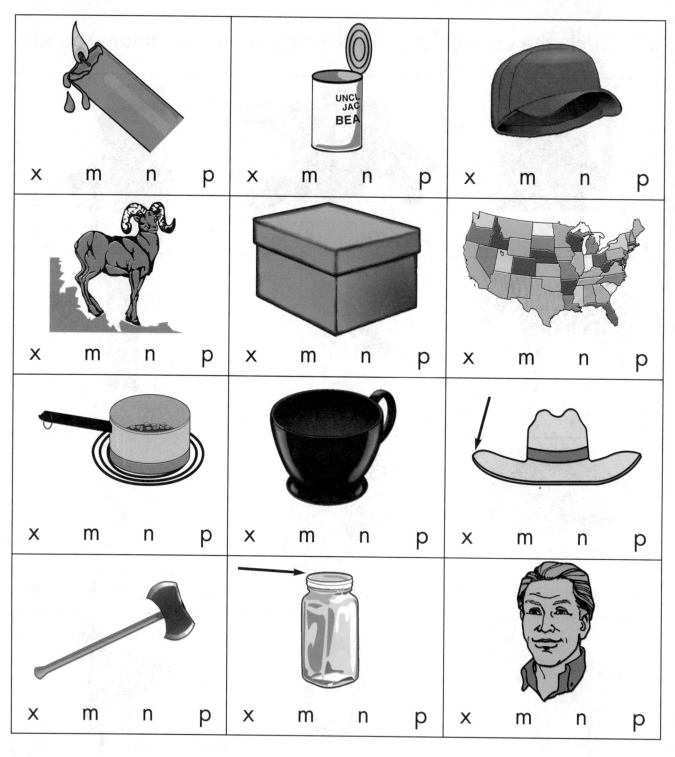

Row 1:
- x m n p
- x m n p
- x m n p

Row 2:
- x m n p
- x m n p
- x m n p

Row 3:
- x m n p
- x m n p
- x m n p

Row 4:
- x m n p
- x m n p
- x m n p

1 Circle the correct letter for the middle short vowel sound.

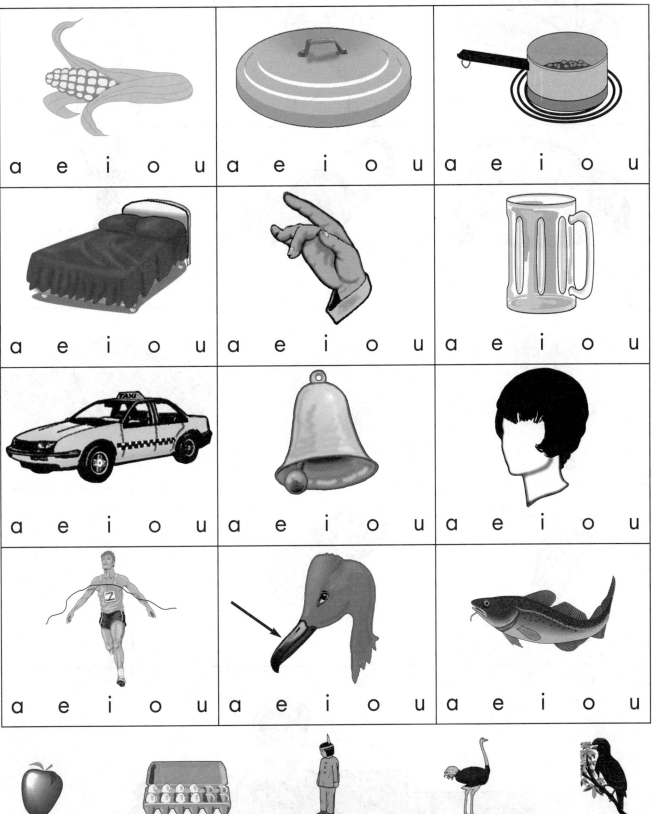

a e i o u   a e i o u   a e i o u

a e i o u   a e i o u   a e i o u

a e i o u   a e i o u   a e i o u

a e i o u   a e i o u   a e i o u

Circle the correct letter for the ending consonant sound.

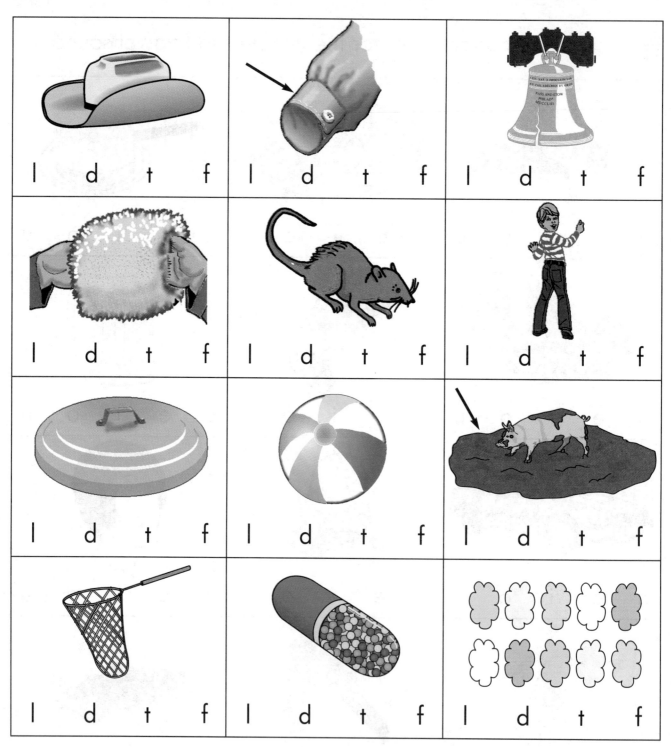

l	d	t	f
l	d	t	f
l	d	t	f
l	d	t	f
l	d	t	f
l	d	t	f
l	d	t	f
l	d	t	f
l	d	t	f
l	d	t	f
l	d	t	f
l	d	t	f

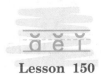
1 Circle the correct letter for the long vowel sound.

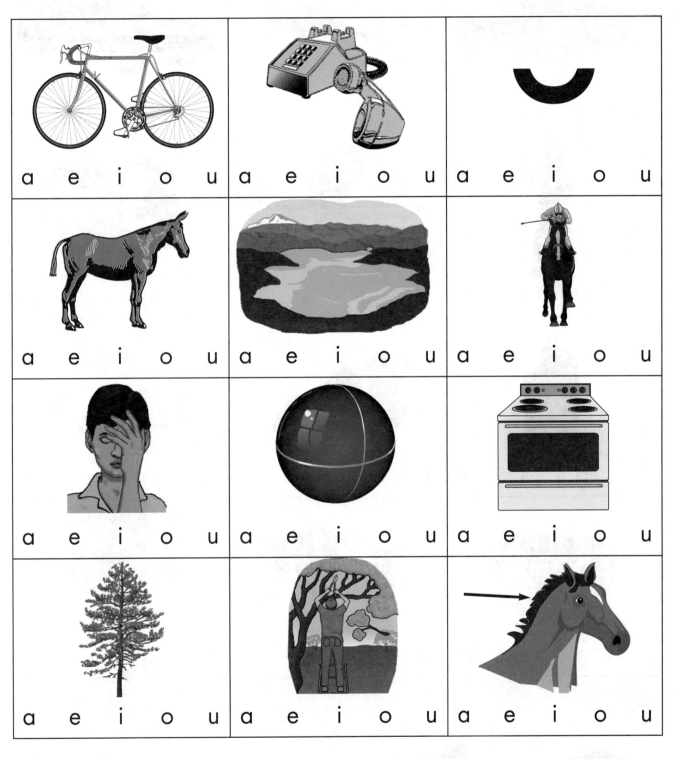

a e i o u   a e i o u   a e i o u

a e i o u   a e i o u   a e i o u

a e i o u   a e i o u   a e i o u

a e i o u   a e i o u   a e i o u

Circle the correct letter for the ending consonant sound.

b g s d	b g s d	b g s d
b g s d	b g s d	b g s d
b g s d	b g s d	b g s d
b g s d	b g s d	b g s d

  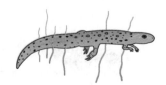 

1 Circle the correct letters for the beginning sound.

ch sh th wh	ch sh th wh	ch sh th wh
ch sh th wh	ch sh th wh	ch sh th wh
ch sh th wh	ch sh th wh	ch sh th wh
ch sh th wh	ch sh th wh	ch sh th wh

2 Circle the correct letter for the short vowel sound.

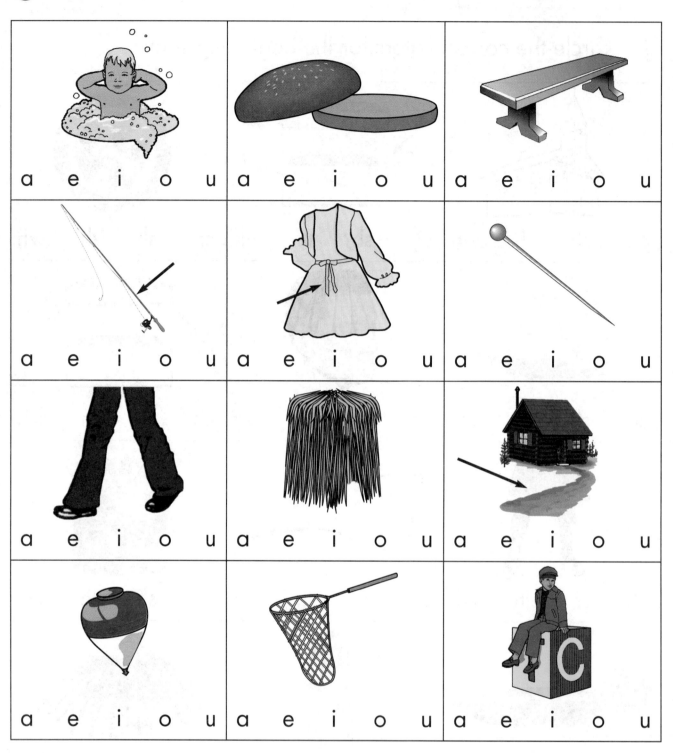

a e i o u   a e i o u   a e i o u

a e i o u   a e i o u   a e i o u

a e i o u   a e i o u   a e i o u

a e i o u   a e i o u   a e i o u

① Circle the correct letters for the ending sound.

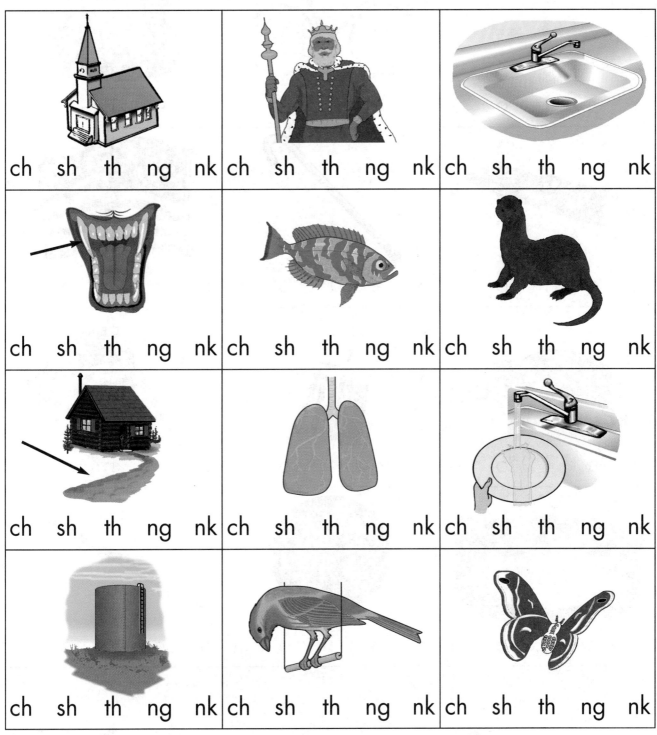

ch sh th ng nk	ch sh th ng nk	ch sh th ng nk
ch sh th ng nk	ch sh th ng nk	ch sh th ng nk
ch sh th ng nk	ch sh th ng nk	ch sh th ng nk
ch sh th ng nk	ch sh th ng nk	ch sh th ng nk

② Circle the correct letter for the long vowel sound.

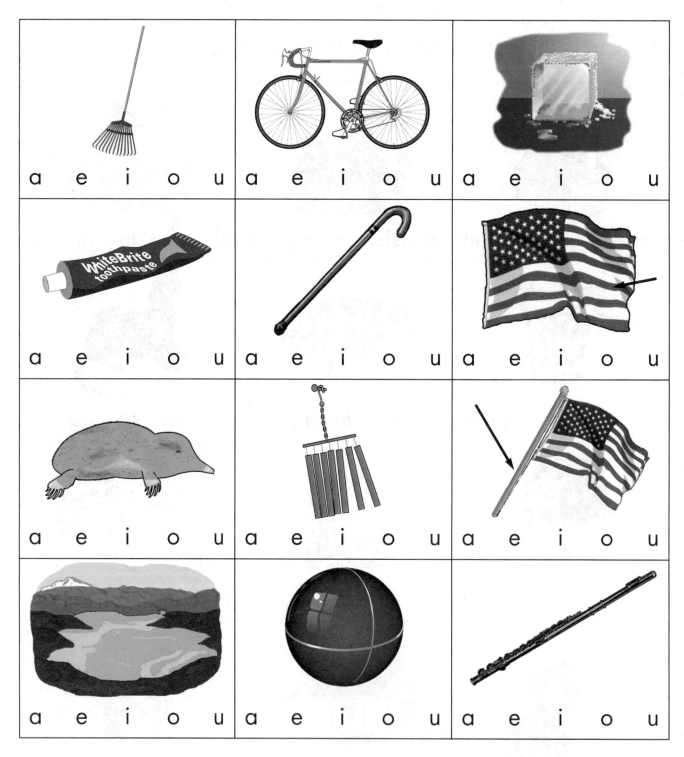

a e i o u   a e i o u   a e i o u

a e i o u   a e i o u   a e i o u

a e i o u   a e i o u   a e i o u

a e i o u   a e i o u   a e i o u

1 Circle the correct letters for the beginning sound.

bl cl fl	bl cl fl	bl cl fl
gl pl sl	gl pl sl	gl pl sl
bl cl fl	bl cl fl	bl cl fl
gl pl sl	gl pl sl	gl pl sl
bl cl fl	bl cl fl	bl cl fl
gl pl sl	gl pl sl	gl pl sl
bl cl fl	bl cl fl	bl cl fl
gl pl sl	gl pl sl	gl pl sl

Circle the letter for the correct vowel sound.

ă / ā	ĕ / ē	ĭ / ī
ŏ / ō	ŭ / ṳ	ă / ā
ĕ / ē	ĭ / ī	ŏ / ō
ŭ / ṳ	ă / ā	ŏ / ō

1 Circle the correct letters for the beginning sound.

br	cr	dr

fr   gr   pr   tr

br	cr	dr

fr   gr   pr   tr

br	cr	dr

fr   gr   pr   tr

br	cr	dr

fr   gr   pr   tr

br	cr	dr

fr   gr   pr   tr

br	cr	dr

fr   gr   pr   tr

br	cr	dr

fr   gr   pr   tr

br	cr	dr

fr   gr   pr   tr

br	cr	dr

fr   gr   pr   tr

br	cr	dr

fr   gr   pr   tr

br	cr	dr

fr   gr   pr   tr

br	cr	dr

fr   gr   pr   tr

② Circle the correct letters for the beginning sound.

sc sk sm sn sp st	sc sk sm sn sp st	sc sk sm sn sp st
sc sk sm sn sp st	sc sk sm sn sp st	sc sk sm sn sp st
sc sk sm sn sp st	sc sk sm sn sp st	sc sk sm sn sp st
sc sk sm sn sp st	sc sk sm sn sp st	sc sk sm sn sp st

1 Circle the letters that make the beginning sound you hear.

dw sw tw	dw sw tw	dw sw tw
dw sw tw	dw sw tw	dw sw tw
dw sw tw	dw sw tw	dw sw tw 12
dw sw tw	dw sw tw	dw sw tw

② Circle the correct letters for the beginning sound.

scr spl	scr spl	scr spl
spr str	spr str	spr str
scr spl	scr spl	scr spl
spr str	spr str	spr str
scr spl	scr spl	scr spl
spr str	spr str	spr str
scr spl	scr spl	scr spl
spr str	spr str	spr str

① Circle the correct letters for the ending sound.

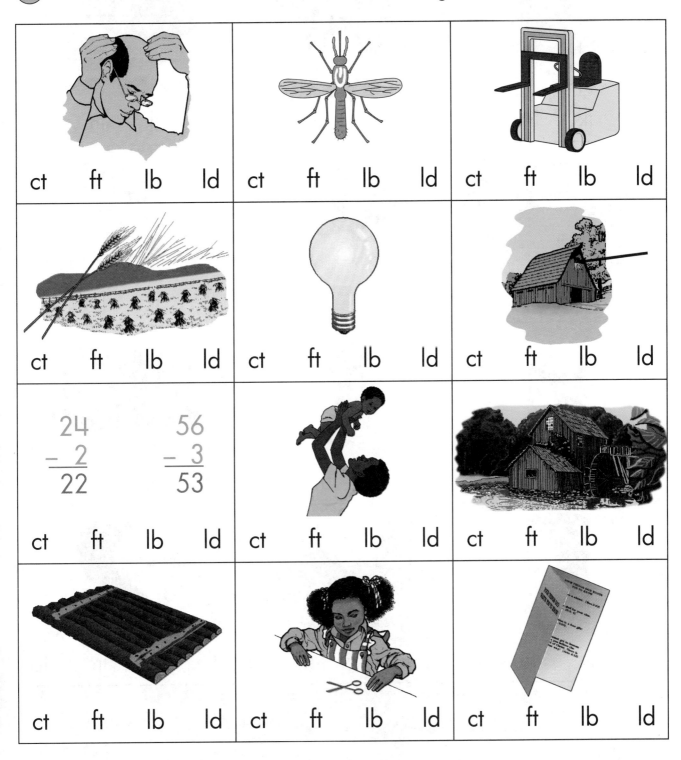

ct	ft	lb	ld
ct	ft	lb	ld
ct	ft	lb	ld

ct	ft	lb	ld
ct	ft	lb	ld
ct	ft	lb	ld

$$\begin{array}{r} 24 \\ -\ 2 \\ \hline 22 \end{array} \qquad \begin{array}{r} 56 \\ -\ 3 \\ \hline 53 \end{array}$$

ct	ft	lb	ld
ct	ft	lb	ld
ct	ft	lb	ld

ct	ft	lb	ld
ct	ft	lb	ld
ct	ft	lb	ld

Circle the correct letters for the ending sound.

lf   lk   lm   lp   lf   lk   lm   lp   lf   lk   lm   lp

lf   lk   lm   lp   lf   lk   lm   lp   lf   lk   lm   lp

lf   lk   lm   lp   lf   lk   lm   lp   lf   lk   lm   lp

lf   lk   lm   lp   lf   lk   lm   lp   lf   lk   lm   lp

1 Circle the correct letters for the ending sound.

lt mp nd nt	lt mp nd nt	lt mp nd nt
lt mp nd nt	lt mp nd nt	lt mp nd nt
lt mp nd nt	lt mp nd nt	lt mp nd nt
lt mp nd nt	lt mp nd nt	lt mp nd nt

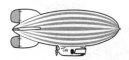

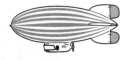

Circle the correct letters for the ending sound.

pt sk sp st	pt sk sp st	pt sk sp st
pt sk sp st	pt sk sp st	pt sk sp st
pt sk sp st	pt sk sp st	pt sk sp st
pt sk sp st	pt sk sp st	pt sk sp st

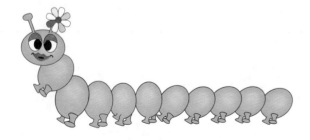

1 Circle the correct letters for the ending sound.

dge lge nge	dge lge nge	dge lge nge
dge lge nge	dge lge nge	dge lge nge
dge lge nge	dge lge nge	dge lge nge
dge lge nge	dge lge nge	dge lge nge

2 Circle the correct letters for the controlled vowel sound.

ar er or	ar er or	ar er or
ar er or	ar er or	ar er or
ar er or	ar er or	ar er or
ar er or	ar er or	ar er or

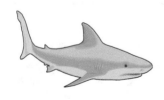

1 Circle the correct letters for the controlled vowel sound.

ar ir or	ar ir or	ar ir or
ar ir or	ar ir or	ar ir or
ar ir or	ar ir or	ar ir or
ar ir or	ar ir or	ar ir or

ar or ur	ar or ur	ar or ur
ar or ur	ar or ur	ar or ur
ar or ur	ar or ur	ar or ur
ar or ur	ar or ur	ar or ur

1   Circle the correct word.

aid **braid** laid	maid paid raid	grail hail jail
tail trail wail	brain chain drain	bait gait wait
taint twain train	mail nail pail	mail nail sail

② Circle the correct word.

pea sea tea	pea peach peak	spear smear shears
hay lay may	day jay fay	stray way tray
bee fee wee	thee tree tee	beep deep jeep

③ Circle the correct word.

creel eel reel	keen queer queen	sleep sheep steep
cheer deer peer	feet fleet feel	wheeze sneeze squeeze
roach coach poach	oak soak oar	coast roast toast

4 Circle the correct word.

boat coat goat	goat coat oat	float gloat throat
load road goad	goad road toad	hoe toe woe
hoe foe toe	bow bowl blown	row sow tow